Acknowledgments

These poems first appeared in the following periodicals:

The American Scholar	First Words
Bloodstone	Honeysuckle
Calyx	The Days Never End
The Christian Science Monitor	At the Window
Commonweal	To My Daughter
Kalliope	Letters to the Chinese Mother of My Daughter
Poetry Northwest	Tantrum
River Oak	Second Father of Our Daughter Telling the Story
Yankee	How You Fall Asleep

"Remorse" was first published in *Essential Love* (Poetworks/ Grayson Books, 2000).
"Answer" was first published in *Touched by Adoption* (Green River Press, 1999).

Published by Poetworks/Grayson Books
Post Office Box 270549
West Hartford, CT 06127

Publisher's Cataloging-in-Publication
(Provided by Quality Books, Inc.)

Siegel, Joan I.
Peach Girl: Poems for a Chinese Daughter/Joan I. Siegel
and Joel Solonche. –1st ed.
p. cm.
ISBN 0-9675554-0-X
1. Adopted children–Poetry.
2. Intercountry adoption–Poetry.
I.Solonche, Joel. II. Title.
PS3569.137475P43 2001   811'.6
QB101-700229

Library of Congress Catalog Card Number: 2001088336

Our special thanks to Jack Heller for designing the cover and pages of this book.

For
Emily Ni Tao,
her family
and her extended family
of aunties, teachers and friends

CONTENTS

The Mother Speaks

CONTENTS

The Father Speaks

*"...my little daughter under the peach
picking a twig of its blossom..."*

–Li Pai

The Mother Speaks

Telling the Story

Of all the stories on your bookshelf
the ones with sadistic step-mothers
and wicked giants
the one I fear most is the story
you will ask me to tell again and again
the story whose beginning I do not know
the one without an ending. What do I tell you
that you will believe
the way you believe the part about fairy godmothers
and kind woodsmen? Should I begin: *Once upon a time*
there was a beautiful Chinese girl. She grew up and
married and had a beautiful baby she loved
more than the world. She named her Peach Girl.
One day the evil prince made her leave the baby
on a hillside shrouded in mist. She cried and
cried for a hundred days and a hundred nights until
she drowned in a river of tears and floated out to sea.
Or should I say: You were luckier than most. Your mother
loved you 14 months before she left you on the roadside. I
don't know what happened to her. *When the mist cleared*
wild cranes dropped from the sky and carried the baby girl
to a far away land where a man and woman dreaming
of the child they could not have
opened their eyes to the sound of wild cranes
and cried for joy when they saw Peach Girl. They lifted her
in their arms and loved her
forever and ever.

To the Chinese Mothers

You
might have drowned
her in the family well,
but her face would come
up to meet yours each time
you filled the bucket.

You
might have slit
her throat,
but you would see
her blood on the knife each time
you sliced a fruit.

You
might have smothered
her with a pillow,
but you would hear her
moan each time
you lay down to rest.

Better
to suffer her birth
again and again
than come to this:

wrap her in quilts and leave
her at some village crossroad
praying to the gods
for good fortune
as before

you
praised them at her birth
counting
ten perfect fingers
ten perfect toes.

Night Benediction

What is it you distill
from the night air
as I lie on your bed
waiting for you to sleep?
You sit on your blankets
tall as a Buddha
hands upturned
floating in the dark
above your knees
lotus petals cupped to the heavens
as though it were raining holy water
and you pour it from one small palm
to the other
touch
anoint my face.

You climb my legs
blind in the dark as a marsupial
groping for the warm pocket of sleep.

Sometimes you tap your head against
the hollow of my belly
as though it were the door of the dark place
where you floated once part mammal part fish.

Falling asleep
sometimes you fall back against me not knowing
but knowing that my body is there
to receive you
the way a branch receives a bird.

Nightmare

Dragons steal your sleep
in far off Zhejiang Province
where it is always the middle of October
in the middle of the night
in the fourteenth month of your life
and your mother carries you on quick feet
up the stone steps of the railway station.

Her face rises like a white moon
above your face.
Her smell is the smell of peach blossom.
Her voice is quiet as pine trees on the mountain.

Her heart rings louder
than a silver bell:
Oh two hearts ringing.

She lays you on a wooden bench.
She puts her lips to yours.
Her feet are quick
down the cold stone steps.

Where is the face of the white moon?
Where is the smell of peach blossom?
Where is the voice of pine trees on the mountain?
Oh one heart
one heart ringing.

Ghost Mother

Is it your hand that tears
her from sleep in the middle of the night
carrying her off to the dead
where she left you
grieving and lost
a thousand nightmares ago?

Her terror shakes the air.
I cannot bring her back
even when she opens her eyes.

Oh, I have mourned you
who must have died of sorrow by now.
But stay where you are.
Stay. Do not haunt her sleep.
Do not haunt the daylight,
the look in her eye when she sees far away.

Two Eyes

My daughter has two different eyes.

I'm never certain
which one is looking back
gathering fist loads of days
colorful as wildflowers and
which one is looking straight ahead.

One drinks up the sun.

The other eye turns down
a sad mouth overcast with rain
a black umbrella.

Letter to My Daughter

I want to tell you
in case there is no time
and you remember only
the smell of air moving
around your sleep
or a shadow falling over your shoulders
weightless as a silk scarf—
how when you are afraid,
you reach for the shiny silver heart
dangling from my throat
and squeeze it in your palm like an amulet,
letting go when your knuckles turn white
and the evil passes.

To keep you safe, I wear
it all the time.

First Words

The way the words push through your lips
sometimes makes me think of the birth of a foal
who squeezes through the dark
a little misshapen and folded
trying to stand on wobbly legs and shake
himself open.

Sometimes you make me think
of a fish feeding on water as you suck in a breath
and out come words like bubbles floating up to the air.

Sometimes you make me think of a glassblower
with his puffy cheeks and eyes squeezed almost shut
intent on the shape turning in the flame.

Sometimes you make me think of a magician
pulling a dove from his sleeve the way you say
bird and it seems to unfold its wings at your mouth
and fly up to a branch on the apple tree.

First Father's Day

Fatherless
who taught you to be
father to this fatherless child
who fills your hand with ten fingers
counting numbers
one by one
as if she were counting petals
fallen from the peonies after rain?

At the Window

My daughter looks like a red poppy
plucked from a field of poppies
sunny in the rain,
the red hood of her jacket bobbing
on her head as she runs to the car,
turns to me,
waves goodbye.

The car pulls away.
My heart is red and full
with a thousand poppies
nodding their heads,
waving
except in that very spot
where she was standing,
where the rain falls.

When You Are Gone from the House

time stops
with your dolls at tea
and the red sock
falling from your bed.

The house fills with you.

My sadness is indecipherable
as the ten blocks circling
a blue crayon on your floor
or the runic lines you drew
across my book.

I pass from room to room
touch nothing
guardian of your temple.

Remorse

My sudden anger darkens your face
and you pull back as though pricked
by thorns in the honeysuckle. You
look at me amazed. For the moment
there is nothing else.
Then we suck in our breath.
Blood rises under your cheeks.
Tears drop from your eyes.
They fall
onto my hands, burning
my skin.

Dandelions

You are bending in the grass
picking dandelions.
You finger each raggedy bloom
and twirl it under the sun.
Soon you will smile at me
and place them
one
by one
in my hands.

I think about your country
where not long ago
you were a bundle left on a roadside
for someone to pick up.

I kneel before you now.
The grass is golden
with dandelions and you.

My Daughter

You are the poem
I cannot write:

the poem of your face
with the blanket pulled over it
when you are far off in sleep
and dressed in the colors of day
when you come back to me

the poem of your feet
stomping
down the hallway
up the stairs
above the roof
over the moon
where you go with a brown cow
on Sundays

the poem of your voice
with its declarations
and questions
the voice of your songs about letters
and numbers and spiders
the spells you cast
in the company of sorcerers and elves
that turn the cat into a dragon
the stones in your palm
into gold

Second Mother

Watching you float
in this warm salt water

rocking between earth and sky
I wonder if you remember

that first ocean where
you floated in the dark

and came ashore on waves
to that first mother

who must now seem ghostly
as this new moon rising.

You do not ask
and I have not the courage

to speak of those apparitions
that trail your sleep:

the humming in your ears
the first taste of milk.

Answer

You want to know who made you.
I can't say
I planted you inside me
like morning glories
we put in the garden last spring.
You grew in another garden,
not mine.
But long ago
you had a sister,
a blind fish
snagged on a root
who made way for you.
Here is the mark on my belly:
a seam crooked as a riverbed.

i

I wonder what is you:

the gesture she makes with her left hand
as though a wild bird just landed
on her wrist

the look in her eyes
when she wakes
as though she were rising
from a deep lake
still wearing the darkness
of the bottom and not yet ready
for the dry air
the brittle light at the surface
where we meet again
after our separate journeys
of the night

how she laughs when she jumps up
so sure the sky will lift her away
and the earth welcome her back

ii

Is it you
taught her how to love
whose fingers touch
when I am sick with fever
and it feels like the sky rained
peonies on my face and
she comes with armloads of drawings
as if she had just gathered all the flowers
in the world for me?

iii

She has not asked about you
but sometimes in the night
she cries in that infant voice
you must still hear in your sleep

Ai ai ai ai ai

I lift her
and she curls into the center of me
as she curled into you
curling back in the dream of a face
looking down on her sleep dreaming
of someone lifting her through the air
speaking the first voice in the world
that holds in it the first smells in the world
the first color of light

Second Father of Our Daughter
(for Joel)

In the middle of the night
her cry pierces your dreams
and you kick off blankets
weighty as sleep and
rush to her room where
I hear you speak
in a language I never thought you knew:
those murmurs
that rock a baby to safety
in the dark when furniture and
stuffed bears prowl the room.

The next morning
you kneel with her in the snow
among bare trees,
filling her hands with seeds
for hungry nuthatches.
Her cheeks are red as apples.
She picks up twigs for the wood stove
and puts them in your hand.

I wonder about
the first father of our daughter:
has he gathered enough winter kindling?

The Days Never End

In our last few minutes
before the school bus comes,
my five-year-old daughter asks:
Do the days ever end? The sun
rises on her forehead.
Halfway around the world
where we first found her,
the sun is setting now.
No, I say kissing her cheeks.
But Mommy — people end, right?
I see all the ancestors of her race
looking at me through her sad
and knowing eyes.
The bus comes.
She climbs on.
She slides into a seat alone.

The bus rolls down the hill,
pulling with it all the days
wound in a tight ball
as I stand behind,
holding this end in my hand.

First Piano Recital

When it came your turn,
you hung your head
like Ping of *The Empty Pot*
unready
to be called to account by the emperor
for having nothing to show
after one year's time—
all the other children's pots
brimming with flowers
while yours had none. Bravely you
walked before the crowd,
the smallest one.
You sat on the bench.
Your black hair shone,
your skin soft as peaches smelled from soap
and powder from the morning's bath.
You closed your eyes
and sucked the air.
Then your fingers
were tendrils on a vine and
suddenly,
all around you,
flowers bloomed.

To the Boy in My Daughter's Class Who Said
She Has to Change Her Eyes

Her eyes are black eyes.
Black eyes hold all the light of the world.
Black eyes give back all the light of the world.
Don't you see two new moons rising
when she looks up at the night sky?
Don't you see your eyes floating in her eyes
like two boats on West Lake?
Don't you feel the wind blowing across the lake
that makes slits of her eyes when she sees far away?
Don't you taste the mist rising from the lake
wetting her cheeks and lashes?
Don't you smell the lotus floating on the water?
Can't you hear the temple gong
ringing from a distant hill?

Halloween Tale

Ghouls and witches
harrow the pumpkin fields
roiling the leaves
startling cornstalks
with their tricks.
My daughter
a princess
sits out the golden afternoon
mute as a swan
and I wonder what terrible raptor
swooped from the trees
ripped laughter from her mouth
what slighted fairy
jealous crone
wreaked such vengeance
not even the magic wand clutched in her hands
can break the spell.

Wild Elephants

Falling asleep
I leave my daughter far behind
in the next room
among the older women of the family.
Their voices weave a magic circle
of incantations around her voice.
Here she dances her dance.
Here she sings her singing
cushioned in bodies
gentle and grey.
Here she will be safe.

Turning Six

We are entering a new country now
and I am homesick for the old one.
This new place of transformations
where serpents with angry
tongues coil in my hair
and suddenly I am a witch,
the thirteenth fairy,
dragon lady.

You
who would be
Rosamund,
Snow White,
Rapunzel,
call for your father
to fly you away
as the sky darkens
and lightning forks the chestnut
outside your window.

Just as suddenly
the sky billows with clouds
white as milk.
You toss your arms
around my neck,
cry, *Mama!*
But your eyes
close warily
warily.

The Blessings of the Grandchild

Even my mother gives up dying
springing out of bed to dance with her

ring around o'rosie

springs in the mattress
bounce on rusty necks

a pocket full o' posie

my father laughs from the dead
where he's been six years

ashes ashes

inside my mother's house
all singing

all fall down!

To My Daughter

When it comes time
let all the words be spoken
that must be
so that I may take your voice with me
for the next ten billion centuries
mine will be with you
like a packet of letters
handwritten over the years
to unfold anytime
read
hear me speak
in the voice that used to put you to bed
telling the story of all our days
fingered in the retelling
like pages of your books
the best parts dog-eared
pressed smooth by thumbprints
and the refrain of all our nights
as you slipped away:
I loved you before dinosaurs
even before the stars

The Father Speaks

Acrostic for Our Daughter, June 1995

Even before you had a name, we began
mothering and fathering the future,
imminent, born twenty months before,
lying bundled, head to foot with another one.
You, our unknown daughter, our Chinese puzzle,

remember always the difficult beginning of us.
Smell the first blossoming flower of being daughter.
First and only daughter, first and only child,
all we had of you we made. We made
a you of a name we loved and many wishes.

Where is Ningbo? You are there.
Come for me to Ningbo, we hear you call.
This way, this way, we hear you call
calling to us from Ningbo, and
to you we call, *Soon we are coming to Ningbo*.

Under a tree I write this poem for you,
and many birds are singing around me,
and I imagine you here under the tree also.
Will you be standing here or there by the peonies?
Did you imagine us, mother and father, and

where we would sit with you there? And did
you imagine also, many birds, many birds
singing around us? I think you hear six
small birds singing around you now,
with your name, Emily, their song.

I Have Spent the Day Saying Father

I have spent the day saying *Father*.
To my wife I have said, *I am going
to be a father*. To the ghost of my
father I have said, *I am going to be
a father*. To the ghost of my wife's
father I have said, *I am going to be
a father*. To myself in the mirror,
I have said, *She is in China,
the daughter of whom I am going
to be the father*. I have stood in front of
the bookshelves, reading the titles
on the spines of the books, finding
A. E. Hotchner's *Papa Hemingway*,
taking it from the shelf and opening
it at random and saying, *I am going
to be a papa*, and finding Turgenev's
Fathers and Sons, taking it from
the shelf and opening it at random
and saying, *I am going to be a father*,
and finally finding *The Father* by
Sharon Olds, taking it from the shelf
and opening it at random and saying,
I am going to be a father. To the ghost
of myself, I have said, *Were you a good
father? What did your daughter learn
from you? What did you learn from
your daughter? What did you pass on?*

Emily's Room

Benjamin Moore semi-
gloss latex enamel super-
white #226-02 on the frame
around her closet   thick
smooth   as heavy cream
smooth   white as vanilla
ice cream melting down
the spoon   after removing
the heavy dark brown
sliding doors   too heavy
for her   replacing them
with louvered bi-folds
much better for two-year
hands   much better for
two-year fingers   the paint
gets on my forty-nine-year
hands   on my forty-nine-
year fingers   and I wipe
them on my paint- wiped
jeans   I do not want
to wash my hands   like
a star-struck teenager
would not after touching
her idol want to ever
again wash her hand
I want to leave a spot
on my knuckle   a spot
under my thumbnail
a spot on the vein that runs
between elbow and wrist
just beneath the surface
just below the body's skin

Beside the Pearl River

in a hotel
with a waterfall
in the lobby,
The White Swan,
my daughter
sleeps between
us in a bed
large enough
for twenty daughters.
My heart is busy
with many feelings,
but in my mind
there are two thoughts,
and then only
one thought:
how the waterfall
and the river
are like father
and daughter:
how a father
of one daughter
is no less a father
than a father
of twenty.

Unlike the Song Poet

Unlike the Song poet
Lin Hejiang,
who spent his life
a bachelor
planting plum trees
and fondling his crane,
I sit in our room
just a stroll
from West Lake,
speaking softly
with my wife,
like the wind
whispering
to the plum tree,
watching my daughter
sleep and the flying
crane of her breathing.
But do not
misunderstand me.
This is not
a regret poem.
This is a great joy poem.

I Am Eating

steamed rice
with my wife
and my daughter.
Nearby
the green water
of the pool
ripples away
under the footbridge
and out of sight.
There could be
a blue butterfly
resting on a
yellow flower petal
on the other side,
slowly folding
and opening
its blue wings.
But since I
have no way
of knowing this,
I have chosen
to believe
there is a blue
butterfly
resting on
a yellow flower
petal on the other
side slowly
folding and
opening its wings.
Here is balance.
Here is happiness
at both ends
of the bridge.

Can You Hear

Can you hear
the beautiful
singing?
I ask you as we
eat supper,
the radio playing
the beautiful
singing of a
Renaissance motet.
But why do I
ask you
this question,
incredible
child, you
who hear all
words as
singing,
you who
hear all sing-
song as beautiful?

Bath

Wars begin like this.

America wants China to take a bath.

It is time for a bath, the time when China has taken a bath
every day for a year.

But today China does not want to take a bath.

America reasons with China: *This is your bath time, we
take a bath every day at this time, you had a bath
yesterday at this time, remember?*

China refuses to take a bath. China says: *I don't wannit.*

America insists. America fills the tub with warm water,
but not too warm water, for China does not like too
warm water.

China says: *I don't wannit.*

America does not care what China says.

America gets China's pink pajamas with the cat motif from
China's drawer.

China does not care about the pajamas.

China says: *I don't wannit.*

America is about to lose patience with China.

America says: *These are your favorite pajamas, you can
wear them after your bath.*

China says: *I don't wannit.*

America loses patience with China.

America is tired of talking about the shape of the table,
the wording of the resolution, the warmth of the
bath water, the color of the pajamas.

America is tired, America wants to lie down and sleep
for a week,
but America is the one and only superpower, and
superpowers cannot lie down, superpowers cannot sleep.

America picks up China by the elbows.

America puts China into the bathtub.

China cries: *I don't wannit, I don't wannit, I don't wannit.*

China kicks her feet, China flails her arms, China
    splashes America.

America considers throwing in the towel.

China is quicker than America.

China throws in the towel.

America lifts the wet towel out of the tub.

America compromises.

America gives China half a bath.

China promises to wash her face later in the sink.

America is no dope.

China bears close watching.

And America is the one and only superpower.

These Dragons

The dragon of my
daughter's dreamful
sleep-life awakens
her in the middle
of the night, and her
awakening awakens
the dragon of my
dreamless life-sleep,
and I spring up,
knowing what has
happened to rush to her.
I reach down, not
knowing what has
happened, into the
shadows her bed is,
and carry her up into
my arms to walk her
and rock her through
the shadows her room
is, so enormously
little, and then to walk
her and rock her through
the shadows of the dim
hallway, and then
to walk her and rock
her back again to her room.
So enormously little
she is, this child. So
enormously little he is,
this man. So enormously
little they are, these dragons.

Tantrum

We know this country.
We know this island continent,
the one you have been visiting so often.
We used to go there, too, when we were your size.

Tell us, daughter, has it changed at all?
Tell us, little traveler, little island-hopper,
is the place as we remember it or not?
It has been so many years since we've been there.

Does the mighty volcano still spew
its red-hot lava down its slopes?
Does it still become that river that boils
its way down to the ocean?

Is it still hot there, hot as a fever in July?
Is the sky still red? Does the air beat in your head
with the pounding *thud thud thud* of an engine?
Does the engine still sound like an elephant's heart?

Do the flowers grow to the size of trees?
Do the trees bear fruit as bitter as medicine?
Is the moon still a bubble, bloated and blue?
Do you still go deaf from the sirenbird's whine?

Tell us, little red-cheeked-as-sunburn-daughter,
is the place as we remember it or not?
Tell us, snorkeler-in-a-sea-of-sob-daughter.
It has been many years since we were there.

You Say Good Night Twenty

You say *good night* twenty
times and mean it, I suppose,
twenty times, and I say *good night*
twenty times in dutiful response
and mean it, I suppose, twenty times,
and when at the twentieth *good night*,
you go to sleep, it is as if you are
feigning sleep, so quick the metamorphosis
from perpetual motion to no motion,
so sudden the collapse to the inert
shape beside me, armless, legless,
round at both ends, a burrower
half-buried in bed-burrow.
Even your breathing seems faked
as I turn over your form from
face-down animal to two-legged,
two-armed person, a cadenced
performance measured to fool
your captured audience.
Too little to fool me because
too little to fool yourself,
you wear no guilty glance or
snaky grin. Your face is calm
to perfection. The future takes
shape there, under cover of darkness.

A Gull

A gull so far
from the river
circles the parking lot.
Its whiteness gleams
in the late fall day's brightness.
Its black edges are lost
in the sunlight.
Its black edges are lost
against the glowing clouds.
My daughter sleeps
in the car and
does not see the gull
gleam above us
so far from the river.
Tomorrow I will have
forgotten the gleam
of the gull that circled
above her so far
from the river.
Years from now
I will have forgotten
to tell her of the gleam
of the gull that circled
above her like a halo,
like a blessing,
as though it had flown
here just for that,
just for her,
so far from the river.

Written with an Aqua Crayon on Yellow Construction Paper
Given Him with Instructions to Write His ABC's

Aqua,
Beautiful
Color,
Daughter
Emily,
For
Giving
Handwriting
Imagination.
Joel's
Kaleidoscopic
Lyric
Means
Nothing,
Only Prepares
Queer
Rarity.
See
Tail
Underneath
Verse?
Wondrous
X-rayed
Yellow
Zebra!

Emily Means

industrious,
which means
she will be our industry,

which means
our life's work
will be the production
of one, one-of-a-kind, unreproducible Emily,

and her
sole industry
will be Emily industriously
making Emily, and thereby beauty,

and thereby
Emily making music
on the piano with
her mother, which means my cottage industry.

Morning Walk with Daughter

Awakening
early and
having to
write a poem

or else suffer
because
in the dream
I had done so

of which
the only words
I remembered
was the word

remember
and the word
November
I took my

daughter
for a long walk
along the streets
in her stroller

noticing only
my daughter's
noticing
of things

and her not
noticing
until I got
over it

and wrote
instead of
that poem
this poem

instead of
suffering
that way
suffer this

My Daughter Asks Me

to rock her to sleep,
so I put down the pen,
and I push aside the paper,
and I take off my glasses
and rub the bridge of my nose
where the nose-pieces
rest and leave their impression,
and I put on my glasses,
and I turn off the light
above my desk,
and I go down the mountain
of the brown-carpeted stairs
into her room,
and I place one of the two stools
from her table by her bed,
and I sit down and reach my hand
over the top of the railing
and rock my daughter to sleep,
and then I get up, put the stool
back by her little table,
touch her cheek, close the door
behind me without a sound,
and I go up the mountain
of the brown-carpeted stairs,
and I turn on the light
over my desk,
and I take off my glasses
and rub the bridge of my nose
where the nose-pieces
rest and leave their impression,
and I put on my glasses
and pull forward the paper,
and I pick up the pen,
and I rock the poem to sleep.

My Daughter Lies

My daughter lies
across my chest. She
is thirty-one inches
and twenty-two pounds.

Her head is the size
of cantaloupes,
or of Chinese roses
in their fullest bloom.

Her hair is feathery
black, and her satin feet
fit in the old leather
shoes of my hands.

She is almost asleep,
but not asleep yet.
Singing herself to sleep,
she will be in a moment.

Not understanding them,
still I know what she sings
are wonderful poems,
for the room is filled

with wonderful poems,
and I am the silent one,
and she, singer of them,
is the one more alone.

Poem That Turns Four Times

On her head, she pulls
down an old hat, the one
we thought too small.
It still covers her ears.

Her hair covers her ears
completely now. That is how
long it is. But she no longer
brushes it away with her hand.

She puts her hand to her brow
to shield her eyes from the sun.
In the car, on her way to become
a citizen, she falls asleep, as usual.

As usual, when she sleeps in
the afternoon, you too sleep.
I lie down but do not sleep.
There is an old hat on my head.

Doing Seventy on the Highway

Doing seventy on the highway,
I look over at my wife.
She is sleeping.
Her head leans against the subtle curve of window.

In my mirrors,
eighteen-wheelers loom up out of nowhere.
They tailgate for a moment,
then spit their headlights and pass.

Each one is a thunderstorm,
splitting the horizon.
White thunderstorm, red thunderstorm,
yellow thunderstorm, green thunderstorm.

I consider doing seventy-five.
I don't. Instead I look back at my daughter.
She is sleeping.
Her head is dropped on her chest.

I reach behind to push up her chin.
Thus far this summer
this is summer's finest day.
The sky is blue right through.

On the hood of my car,
the sun does a golden dance.
Tell me what the speed of darkness is.
I have to go faster.

Sweeter

Sweeter than
the lilac while
you and Emily

plant flowers
in the pots
on the patio

she repeating
your instructions
as you give them

learning for
next spring
by heart

this ritual
dance of hands
and plants and

pots and roots
and dirt and the
garden hose's

benediction
of spray spills
over us sweeter

than the lilac
O praise the future
filled with daughter

Prayer

O god of daughters,
Guard well this daughter,
Guard well this daughter

With the thick-calloused
Palm of your right hand.
Guard well this daughter

With the power of your
Male voice, thunder-loud,
Thunder-profound.

Guard well this daughter
With your chest's
Broad expanse, resilient

As the shield
Of the stretched bull-hide.
Guard well this daughter

With the sinews of your thighs
As the temple-columns
Carry the roof of the temple.

Guard well this daughter
With the stern gaze
Of your eye, ablaze ever,

Focused as lightning,
Incorruptible as gold.
O god of daughters,

Guard well this daughter,
For the hand of this daughter's father
Is as weak as the grass,

And his voice is as thin
As the breath in the shepherd's pipe,
And his chest is as narrowly small

As the breast of the sparrow,
And his thighs are as slender
As the reeds by the bank of the river,

And the gaze of his eye
Is doubtful and dim
And lost in the dark.

Honeysuckle

By the road,
at the bottom of the driveway,
you pick honeysuckle flowers.
You pluck the white, silk-smooth, heart-shaped petals
and strew them on the ground at your feet.
You tell me to do the same,
so I pick the honeysuckle flowers,
pluck the white, silk-smooth, heart-shaped petals
and strew them on the ground with yours.

I marvel at how much you have grown
in a year. You are as tall as a yardstick.
You can reach all of the doorknobs,
most of the light switches,
half of the faucets.
I grunt now when I pick you up.

But it is another summer I think of,
a summer as far off as another planet,
yet a summer that will arrive as swift
as an arrow toward the heart,
as straight as an arrow into the heart,
as sharp as an arrow through the heart.

You are at the bottom of the driveway,
with a boy your age or older,
and you pick honeysuckle flowers,
pluck the petals, strew them on the ground at your feet.
You tell him to do the same,
so he picks honeysuckle flowers,
plucks the petals, strews them on the ground with yours,
white, silk-smooth, little hearts.

Swimming Lesson

Your hair is plastered to your head.
Your pigtails drip,
two black icicles in the sun.

You wipe water from your face
with one hand. With the other,
you grip the handhold.

You wait for your turn to float
on your back or stomach
or kick with the yellow board.

You are small there,
up to your shoulders in water,
but you are not afraid.

Daughter, listen carefully.
No matter what you may read
or what you may hear,

this water is no metaphor for life,
nor this lesson one for learning how to live.
Daughter, listen more carefully.

I am about to contradict myself.
One day you will wipe life from your face.
One day you will grip the handhold.

One day you will await your turn
to float on your back or stomach
or kick with the yellow board.

One day you will be small there,
up to your shoulders in it.
But you will not be afraid.

Daughter, now listen
most carefully of all.
I say you will not be afraid.